The Battle of Bloreheath
1459

The Battle of Bloreheath 1459

The First Major Conflict of the Wars of the Roses

Francis Randle Twemlow

LEONAUR

The Battle of Bloreheath 1459
The First Major Conflict of the Wars of the Roses
by Francis Randle Twemlow

First published under the title
The Battle of Bloreheath

Leonaur is an imprint of Oakpast Ltd

Copyright in this form © 2011 Oakpast Ltd

ISBN: 978-0-85706-475-2 (hardcover)
ISBN: 978-0-85706-476-9 (softcover)

http://www.leonaur.com

Contents

Dedication

To Colonel Sir Philip Walhouse Chetwode,
Baronet, D.S.O., of Oakley co. Stafford, and
Chetwode co. Bucks.,
late commanding the 19th
(Queen Alexandra's Own Royal) Hussars,
the present owner
of the historic soil of Bloreheath,
this Book is dedicated.

Introductory

PREVIOUS ACCOUNTS. During the nineteenth century various accounts of this battle were written, the four following authors being perhaps the best known:—

1. Rev. W. Snape, Curate of Keele and Maer, who wrote in the *Gentleman's Magazine* of December 1812, and whose article is quoted in Pitt's *History of Staffordshire* (published in 1817).
2. Mr. W. Beamont, who read a paper before the Chester Archaeological Society in 1850.
3. Mr. Richard Brooke, F.S.A., who read a paper before the Society of Antiquaries of London in December, 1853; and published it, along with accounts of other battles, in 1857.
4. Professor Charles W. Oman, F.S.A., Fellow of All Souls' College, Oxford, Chichele Professor of Modern History, in his *Warwick the King-maker*, which appeared in 1891.

With regard to these:—

1. Mr. Snape thought that on the night before the battle, Lord Audley and the Lancastrian army were at Camp Hill, and the Earl of Salisbury and the Yorkists at Byrth Hill, both of which places are at Maer, five miles to the North-east of Bloreheath. He thought that the "pass" mentioned by the Chronicler Rapin was at the foot of the Byrth Hill, and that Salisbury's feigned retreat was continued all the way from there to Audley's Cross on Bloreheath, near which place he admits that the battle took

place.

All this seems very unnecessary and improbable; for, to begin with, had Salisbury taken this line, he would not have been re-treating at all, but on the contrary advancing on his way to Lud-low. And besides this, the "pass" can be found close to Audley's Cross, without going five miles to look for it.

2. Mr. Beamont quotes the Chroniclers Stow, Baker, Holin-shed, Rapin, and also Dr. Lingard's account, based upon the au-thority of Hall and Whethamstede. He also gives much valuable information about mediaeval commissariat arrangements. But, as regards the actual fighting, he seems to have been misled by local tradition into supposing that, before the battle, Audley was encamped at Audley Brow, near Moreton Say, five miles to the West of Bloreheath, (but with his army on Little Drayton Com-mon three miles away from him); and Salisbury on Salisbury Hill, one mile to the South of Market Drayton, and three miles away from the battlefield.

This tradition about the camps at Audley Brow and Salisbury Hill seems to have prevailed at any rate as early as the mid-dle of the eighteenth century, but is clearly wrong. For in the first place, Audley Brow was called "Audley" in the thirteenth century, two hundred years or more before the battle (Eyton's *History of Shropshire*, vol. ix.), and the name is in no way con-nected with the fight. And, secondly, Salisbury had his camp on Salisbury Hill, not *before* the battle, but *after* it. The Parliamentary Rolls tell us that he was at Drayton the day after the battle, and left his wounded behind there; and there seems to be no room for doubt about the matter.[1]

Mr. Beamont, however, having adopted this theory, and, for reasons which are rather hard to follow, having rejected the natural and simple idea that the two armies were encamped at Bloreheath, on opposite sides of the Hempmill brook; proceeds to give his notion of what happened.

He invites us to believe that, on the day before the battle,

---

1. See the bill of impeachment from the Parliamentary Rolls, 38 Hen.VI.Vol.V. fo. 348, quoted by Mr. Brooke, p. 33.

Salisbury divided his small force; leaving behind one portion at Bloreheath to form an ambuscade there, and pushing on with the remainder to Salisbury Hill. We are then to suppose that with these advanced troops, after discharging a flight of arrows into the enemy's camp on the other side of the Tern, he retired by way of Peatswood, the Hills Farm, and Almington, to draw the Lancastrians into the trap; and that, after a pursuit extending over three miles of broken country, they came up with him just where he intended.

The obvious comment is that it is most unlikely that an experienced General like Salisbury would have had his small force divided at night time, detaching part of it on something very like a wild goose chase; that he should have followed at dawn with the remainder, taking a bee-line across two boggy valleys and a wood, disregarding all roads and fords, when pursued by a force of more than twice his strength, which commanded the ordinary road between his point of departure and his destination; and still more unlikely is it that, having done all this, he should have been rewarded by a crushing victory.

Mr. Beamont has been followed by a later writer, Mr. C. R. B. Barrett, who, in his *Battles and Battlefields of England*, has a chapter on Bloreheath. The unlikely story that Salisbury had his camp at Salisbury Hill before the battle, and retired from there to Bloreheath pursued by Audley, is there repeated. It was also adopted by Miss F. M. Wilbraham, in her historical novel *Queen Margaret's Badge*, and has obtained wide currency.

3. Mr. Brooke's paper may or may not have been intended as a reply to Mr. Beamont's. He assumes, no doubt correctly, that the opposing armies were facing each other on Bloreheath, with the Hempmill brook between them; that the feigned flight took place there, and did not go very far; and that the fighting all took place within a small area.

Mr. Brooke gives most valuable quotations from contemporary records, and much information about the leading men of the time, and pedigrees illustrating their relationships. But his account of the actual fighting is very condensed, extending to only twelve lines of large print. He visited the battlefield twice before he read his paper, and four times subsequently before he published his book. And he knew nothing of local matters, except what he picked up from some of the tenant farmers.

4. Professor Oman, as we should expect, throws much new light upon the matter. He was acquainted with the contemporary chronicles of William Gregory and Jehan de Waurin,[2] both of which were unknown to the previous writers. These chronicles give interesting particulars as to the nature of the fighting, and the character of the ground, from which deductions may be drawn. The Professor, however, was writing about Warwick, who was not present at Bloreheath; and was not concerned to go deeply into the matter. He did not visit the battlefield; and his account of the battle is a brilliant sketch condensed within the limits of a single page.

AIM OF THE PRESENT WRITER. It can therefore scarcely be said that the ground has been fully covered, and that there is no more to be said on the subject. The present writer does not pretend to be an authority either about military matters or antiquities; but as regards this particular battle he has enjoyed certain advantages, which may perhaps be held to justify his taking up the pen. In the first place, he has lived near the battlefield for more than thirty years, and knows both it and the surrounding neighbourhood intimately. And, secondly, he has for the last eight years been an enthusiastic student of local history, having examined and noted every document connected with the Manor of Tyrley that he could find, either in public collections or in private hands; and by so doing has accumulated a considerable mass of parochial information, some of it extending back to quite early times.

By comparing this with the statements of the Chroniclers, and with the treatises on mediaeval warfare, it has been possible to arrive at certain conclusions with regard to the Battle of Bloreheath, which are here set down.

---

2. See Appendices A and B *infra*.

It is hoped that this little book may be of interest, at any rate to residents in the neighbourhood; and also that it may incite others to undertake work of the same kind, and to do it better.

CHAPTER 1

Audley's Cross

The Battle of Bloreheath was fought on St. Tecla's Day, Sunday 23rd September 1459.

The combatants were, on the one side, a Yorkist army of about 5,000 men, commanded by Richard Neville Earl of Salisbury, which was marching from Middleham Castle in the North Riding of Yorkshire, to effect a junction with their friends at Ludlow; and on the other, a Lancastrian force of some 10,000 hastily collected men under James Touchet Lord Audley, which had been got together to oppose it.

The only surviving memorial of the battle is the Stone Cross known as "Audley's Cross," which is supposed to mark the spot where Lord Audley was killed; and which stands in a field on the South side of the road leading from Newcastle-under-Lyme to Market Drayton, about two miles and a-half from the latter place. It is in the Manor of Tyrley, which includes all the Staffordshire part of Market Drayton parish. Tyrley is now a civil parish.

The existing cross was repaired in 1765, as the inscription on it records; but it is likely that a cross was set up here very soon after the battle. Dr. Plot writing in 1686 mentions it, and calls it an "antiquity."

And we learn from a Court Roll of Tyrley Manor that a field adjoining the heath on which the cross stood was known as the "Barn Cross" so long ago as 1553. The farm now known as the Audley Cross Farm is comparatively modern, having been built subsequently to the enclosure of the heath in 1775.[1] Before that time there was upon its site only a small holding of about six acres, known as the "Squab," and which had been formed by some squatter in the middle of the unenclosed waste. A mound near this farmhouse has been supposed by some people to mark a burial place; but I do not know that there is any evidence to support this conjecture.

---

1. Under the provisions of an Act passed in 1773.

CHAPTER 2

Summary of Events Between 1422 and 1459

In order to understand the battle, it is necessary to bear in mind the political conditions of the time, and the leading events of the years immediately preceding, which may be briefly summarised as follows:

During the reign of Henry VI. the Royal power was in the hands of the Privy Council. This was necessarily so at first, during the minority of the young King, but Henry's character rendered him unfit at any time to exercise personal control over the affairs not only of England, but also of France, in those warlike days. He was upright, conscientious, unselfish, and devout; but he suffered from bodily weakness, and from attacks of mental imbecility, the last being inherited from his maternal grandfather King Charles VI. of France. So long as the Duke of Bedford, Henry's uncle, survived, the Government was in capable hands; but after his death in 1435 this was no longer the case.

And in the years that followed, the English ascendancy in France was totally lost. The Council was divided into two factions, one led by Cardinal Beaufort and William de la Pole Earl of Suffolk, the other by Humphrey Duke of Gloucester the King's uncle, and Richard Duke of York the King's cousin and heir presumptive. Suffolk arranged the truce with France in 1444, and the marriage of the King with Margaret of Anjou in 1445; and in 1447 the deaths of Beaufort and Gloucester, and the removal of York to Ireland, rendered him completely master of the situation. The failure of his foreign policy, and the loss of Normandy, brought about his fall and death in 1450; and the Duke of York became the spokesman of the national discontent. In addition to his high rank, he was a man of experience and of approved worth both in war and administration: and up to this time he had shown no inclination to push his hereditary claim to the Crown (which was better than Henry's), but was patiently waiting for the inheritance to come to him in the natural course of events.

But in 1453, more than eight years after the marriage of Henry and Margaret, the birth of a Prince of Wales disappointed his expectations, and materially altered his position for the worse. In 1454, during the King's illness, he was appointed Protector, but on the recovery of Henry a year later he found himself deprived of all authority. This led him to resort to force; and the first battle of St. Albans restored him to power, but made the quarrel between him and the Queen irreconcilable. His chief supporters were his brother-in-law Richard Earl of Salisbury, and the latter's son Richard Earl of Warwick (known in history as the "King-maker").

The Queen relied principally on the Dukes of Somerset and Exeter, the Earls of Wiltshire and Shrewsbury, and Viscount Beaumont. In 1457, by the efforts of King Henry, the Queen and the Duke of York were brought together and a pacification effected between them; but this was more apparent than real, and in 1458 further trouble ensued.

Warwick, who was Governor of Calais, had been summoned to London to account for his proceedings there; and in Westminster was set upon by the retainers of Somerset and Wiltshire, so that he barely escaped with his life. This attack was supposed by the Yorkists to have been arranged by the Queen. After this both sides organised their forces and prepared for war. The Queen made a progress through Lancashire and Cheshire, taking her infant son with her, and distributing liveries of the silver swan amongst her adherents. The Yorkist headquarters were at

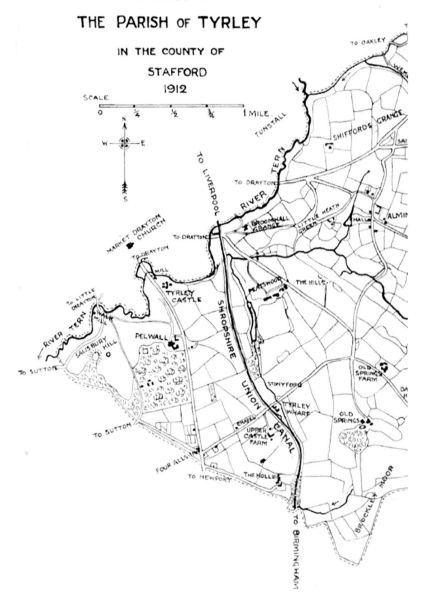

PLAN OF
THE PARISH OF TYRLEY
IN THE COUNTY OF
STAFFORD
1912

SCALE

0   ¼   ½   ¾   1 MILE

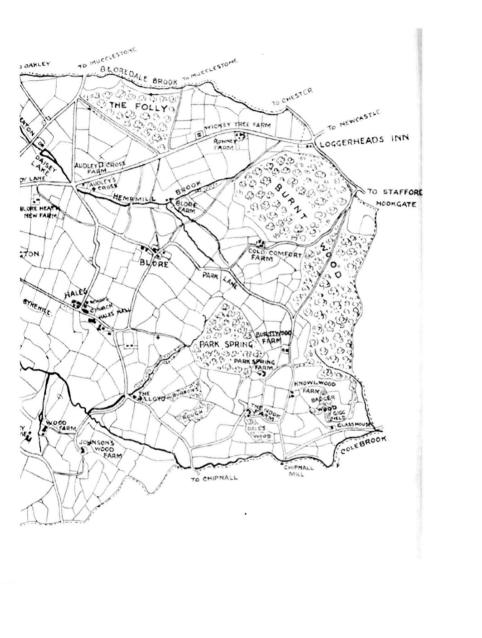

Ludlow, where the Duke himself was. Ludlow was his private property, as heir of the great Marcher family of Mortimer, and he had also the important Castle of Wigmore in the same district. Salisbury's strength lay in the North Riding of Yorkshire, and he was at his Castle of Middleham. Warwick was back again at Calais, where he could command considerable force, both by sea and land.

Matters were brought to a head by the dispatch of a summons to Salisbury, ordering him, in the King's name, to come to London. To do so would have been to place himself in the hands of his enemies; so he naturally disobeyed, and proceeded with some 3,000 of his tenantry to join his friends at Ludlow. Warwick was told to do the same; and though he had to pass through a hostile region, succeeded in arriving there without fighting.

CHAPTER 3

Salisbury and His Army

(A) *The Yorkist Leader.* With regard to the personality of the Earl of Salisbury and the quality of his troops, it must be remembered that Richard Neville was 60 years of age, having been born in 1399, and that he was the son of Ralph Neville Lord of Raby and Middleham, who was in charge of the Scottish border in the reigns of Henry IV. and V., and who was created Earl of Westmorland. Ralph was twice married; by his first wife Margaret Stafford he had nine children, and by his second wife Joan Beaufort he had fourteen, including six sons, of whom Richard was the eldest. Richard saw some service in France in his young days, but he does not seem to have been engaged in the later disastrous campaigns.

In 1425 he married Alice Montacute, daughter and heiress of the Earl of Salisbury; and on the death of his father-in-law, who was killed before Orleans in 1428, he succeeded to the title and estates. In 1433 he was, according to Lord Campbell,[1] Lord of the East and West Marches of Scotland; and in the following year he was retained by indenture to serve in France with a contingent of three *bannerets*, seven knights, two hundred and forty-nine men-at-arms, and a thousand and forty archers, but it does not appear that he was actually called upon to go.

Professor Oman has explained in his *Warwick the King-maker* that there was bitter discord between old Ralph Neville's two families over the division of the inheritance; the second one

---

1. Lives of the Lord Chancellors.

having, with the assistance of their mother, secured the lion's share. And in 1435 there was actual fighting going on between them in Yorkshire. In 1436, Salisbury, with his brother-in-law York, went on a futile embassy to France. And after his return in 1437, he was made a Privy Councillor; an appointment which he held for the next ten years, and which kept him busy in London for the most part during that period. After that, he again turned his attention to war and recruiting.

Professor Oman quotes a deed executed by him and Sir Walter Strykelande, Knight, in September 1449, whereby the latter placed himself and his retinue of nearly 300 men at the service of the Earl, and in his pay, against all folk saving his allegiance to the King. This agreement was perhaps only one of many, which would account for the rapid mobilisation of the Yorkshire forces in 1455, whereby the first battle of St. Albans was won. In that battle Salisbury took a leading part, and must have added to his military knowledge in a sufficiently practical manner.

He was Lord Chancellor for a short time during the Duke of York's Protectorate in 1454-5; but it does not appear that he shone as a legal luminary.

One other point as regards his family relationships and his connection with the owner of Tyrley Manor. The Lord of Tyrley at this time was John Neville, of Oversley near Alcester. His father was Ralph Neville, second son of old Earl Ralph and Margaret Stafford. Consequently we should anticipate that John would not be friendly towards his half-uncle Richard. But John's mother was Mary Ferrers, who was daughter, by her first husband Robert Ferrers, of the very same Joan Beaufort who was Salisbury's mother. This fact may possibly have influenced his feelings in the opposite direction; and as the result he may have decided to be strictly neutral. At any rate, so far as I know, there is no evidence that he took a decided line one way or the other. His father Ralph had died in 1458, his mother having died previously; and he then succeeded to Tyrley. But he was not in possession of it when he died in 1483; and he seems to have handed it over to his grandson in his lifetime.

(B) *The Yorkist Army*. The most circumstantial account which we have of Salisbury's army is given by Waurin, who says that it consisted of about twenty-five knights and from six to seven thousand armed men (*hommes deffensables*), of whom not more than forty were men-at-arms, that is heavy cavalry. The estimate is perhaps rather high, both as to knights and rank and file. The Act of Attainder passed by the Lancastrian partisan Parliament, which met at Coventry in this same year, gives the names of five knights only and two esquires. These were Sir John and Sir Thomas Neville, Salisbury's sons, Sir Thomas Harrington,[2] his son-in-law, Sir John Conyers, and Sir Thomas Parr; with Thomas Mei ing, of Tong in Yorkshire, and William Stanley (af terwards Sir William), esquires.[3] The Act of Attainder gives the number of men with them as above five thousand, and there is no doubt that, besides the men who started from Middleham, others joined during the march.

The force had carts with it, so probably it carried some supplies, as well as equipment, and was not wholly dependent for subsistence upon the country through which it passed. It had no artillery,[4] nor does it seem to have relied upon firearms of any kind, though we do hear of some blank firing during the night after the battle. With regard to training and discipline, the Yorkshiremen, or some of them, may have taken part in the battle of St. Albans four years before, and they had no doubt had experience of fighting, and looting, on the Scottish border. We may be sure that they knew how to handle their weapons; and the march of over 100 miles, through a difficult country, must have been of great value in accustoming officers and men to work together as component parts of an organised body.

As to the route taken from Middleham, we have no very precise information. Mr. Beamont says that it was through Cra-

---

2. Sometimes called Lord Harrington. He had married Salisbury's daughter Katherine. He was killed at Wakefield.
3. Sir Roger Kynaston, who is supposed to have killed Lord Audley, is not in this list. But he may have been present, and was certainly at Ludford, subsequently. Blakeway's *Sheriffs of Shropshire*.
4. There were guns at Ludlow.

ven (that is the part of the North Riding in which the River Aire rises), and South Lancashire; and from Manchester by Congleton to Newcastle-under-Lyme. The wording of the Act of Attainder passed by the Parliament at Coventry implies that Salisbury changed his plans and altered his line of march in consequence of the resistance which was threatened to his progress. And it is evident that his direct road to Ludlow would have been through the middle of Cheshire, and by Whitchurch, Wem, and Shrewsbury, and not by Newcastle and Market Drayton. The Parliamentary Rolls give the distance from Newcastle to Bloreheath as six miles only; but it is nearly twelve. The tendency of old writers was to underestimate mileage.

CHAPTER 4

Audley and His Army

Leaving the Yorkist army within a day's march of the scene of conflict, let us now turn to the other side, and see what measures had been taken to bar its progress.

(A) *The Lancastrian Leader.* James Touchet, Lord Audley, the Lancastrian general, was a man who had inherited great possessions in Staffordshire, Shropshire, and Cheshire. His Staffordshire estates lay round the Manor from which he took his title, and his neighbouring Castle of Heleigh. His Shropshire seat was the Red Castle at Hawkstone. In Cheshire he had Newhall Tower, near Combermere, and a considerable portion of the old barony of Nantwich. All these were ancient possessions of the Audley family, and had come to him through his great-grandmother Joan de Audley, who married Sir John Touchet in the reign of Edward III. And in addition he had inherited from his father's family the Manor of Buglawton, near Congleton, in the Macclesfield Hundred of Cheshire; besides lands at Markeaton and other places in Derbyshire.

Born in 1400, he attained his majority and was summoned to Parliament in 8th Hen.V. (1421); and Ormerod says of him (*History of Cheshire*,Vol. III.):

> The Lords Audley had now arrived at a pitch of power and influence which causes their personal history henceforward to relate more nearly to the annals of the kingdom at large, than to those of the county of their ancestors.

He served in France under Henry V., and returned to England with the King's body in 1422. And he had a command in France in 1431. He was twice married, first to Margaret daughter of Lord Cobham, by whom he had two daughters; and secondly to Eleanor, natural daughter of Edmund Holland Earl of Kent, by the Lady Constance Plantagenet daughter of Edmund Langley Duke of York. Eleanor endeavoured to prove that her father and Lady Constance were married, and that she herself was legitimate, and the sole heiress of her father's lands; which brought her into collision with her father's sisters and others, who had divided his property between them.

These co-heiresses and their representatives included the Duchesses of York and Clarence, the Duke of York, and the Earls of Westmorland and Salisbury; who, fearing that they might lose their estates, preferred a Bill in Parliament 9 Henry VI. (1431) against Eleanor Lady Audley, upon which she was declared to be the offspring of "pretended espousals," and consequently entitled to nothing. So that Lord and Lady Audley had a grievance of long standing against the Duke of York and both branches of the Neville family.[1]

After this we hear no more of Audley till 1457, when he received a commission to summon, if necessary, the Sheriff and *Posse Comitatus* of Herefordshire to suppress any designs formed by the King's enemies in that county.[2] Mr. Beamont thinks that this commission led to his further employment in 1459. But, whether that was so or not, we can understand that Queen Margaret would trust him, not only because of his long fidelity to the house of Lancaster, but also on account of his old grudge against the Yorkist leaders, which could hardly be forgiven, or forgotten. Whatever the reasons for the selection may have been, Audley was chosen by the Queen to uphold her cause in the Midland Counties in September, 1459.

(B) *The Lancastrian Army.* How much time he had in which

---

1. Chetwynd's *History of Pirehill Hundred*, Salt Collections, Vol. XII. N.S. And Harwood's *Erdeswick*. 2. The Duke of York's Castle of Wigmore was in Herefordshire; and much of his strength lay in the Welsh Marches.

to prepare is not stated; but he must have made good use of it, in order to bring 10,000 men into line at the right spot at the right moment. He would no doubt summon the tenants from his own estates to muster[3]; and they would probably do so at his three Castles of Heleigh, Hawkstone, and Newhall. From thence they might naturally proceed to Market Drayton, and concentrate there. Drayton is centrally placed, and not more than ten miles from any one of the Castles. It had the further advantage of being held by an unwarlike Lord, the Abbot of Combermere. And, as for the neighbouring Castle of Tyrley, it had little strength or importance, and its Baron had presumably no great love for his relative, the Yorkist general.

Audley's army was numerous, and it was strong in cavalry. As to the nobility and knights who served with it, we have no complete list. But we know who were killed and the names of some of the prisoners, and these formed a large proportion of those who were engaged. The second in command was John

3. With regard to the process of mobilisation, the following Covenant in a lease is instructive. It relates to a hundred acre farm in Betchton, a Cheshire Manor of which the Lords Audley were tenants in *capite*, and the Davenports of Henbury *mesne* lords, in the 15th and 16th centuries. The lease in question dates from Queen Elizabeth's reign; but the Covenant had no doubt been handed down from earlier days, and the same wording continued to be used by the Wilbrahams, who succeeded the Davenports as lords of Betchton, as late as 1646. And the Wilbrahams have still, at Delamere, some armour which was intended for the equipment of their retinue. It shows that the Cheshire tenantry were bound by covenant to be prepared for war, and that when their feudal lord served personally, more was expected of them than when the Sheriff made a general levy.

Covenant. "And when and so often as the said Randle Davenport or his heirs shall within the said term be appointed to serve the Queen's majesty her heirs or successors in the wars in his or their proper person That then the said John Ellison if he be then living or able to serve or otherwise his assign or assigns shall in his or their proper person be ready furnished with armour and weapons to serve under and in the Retinue of the said Randle Davenport or his heirs in the same wars. Also when and so often as the said Randle Davenport or his heirs shall within the said term be compelled to set forth or furnish any men within the lordship of Betchton aforesaid for and towards the same wars that then the said John Ellison or his assigns shall and will procure or find one sufficient man unfurnished to serve in the said wars at the appointment of the said Randle Davenport or his heirs or shall contribute in money or otherwise to the said Randle Davenport and his heirs as others then tenants of the same Randle of the like rent shall hereafter do."

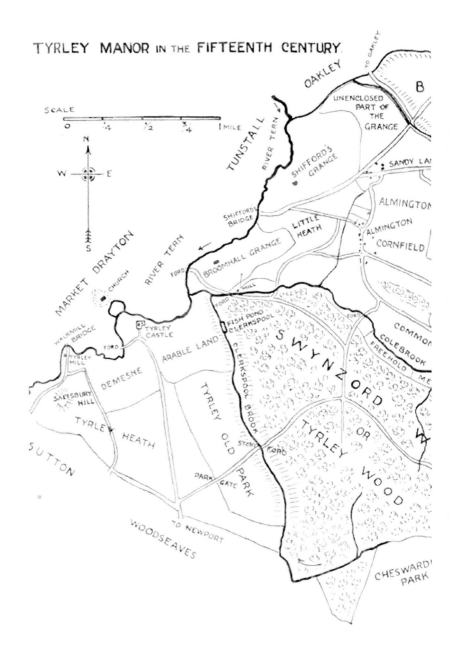

TYRLEY MANOR IN THE FIFTEENTH CENTURY.

TO MUCCLESTONE

BLOREDALE

LORE HEATH

TO NEWCASTLE

ROUNHAY WOOD

ASHLEY PARISH

DUDLEY CROSS

NETHERBLORE

THE DEFILE

BLOREHEATH MILL

OALACRE

MEADOWS

BLORE

ECCLESHALL PARISH

BROUGHTON TOWNSHIP

HALES
CORN

BLORE
CORN
FIELD

PARK LANE

FIELDS

HALES

TYRLEY NEW PARK

CHAPEL

MEADOWS

KNOWL·WOOD

COLEBROOK
CHIPNALL
MILL

FORD

Heath lands are coloured Yellow.

Arable lands are coloured Pink.

The Red and Blue lines show the supposed positions
of the Lancastrian and Yorkist armies at the
Battle of Bloreheath, 23rd September, 1459.

Sutton, Lord of Dudley in South Staffordshire, and also of Malpas in Cheshire. He was a man of distinction, having carried the Standard at the funeral of Henry V., and acted as Lieutenant of Ireland, and in other capacities, for Henry VI. He was no friend to the Duke of York, who had imprisoned him twice, in 1449 and in 1455[4]. There were also serving Sir Robert de Booth, of Dunham; Sir Hugh Calveley, Sir John Done (Donne, or Dunne), of Utkinton (or Wickington), Cheshire, hereditary forester of Delamere Forest, whose younger brother Hugh married Lord Audley's daughter; Sir Robert Downes, of Shrigley, near Macclesfield; Sir Thomas Dutton, of Dutton, son-in-law of Lord Audley; Sir John Egerton, of Egerton; Sir John Legh, of Booths; Sir Richard Molineux, of Sefton, and Sir William Troutbeck, of Dunham-on-the-Hill, both of whom had married daughters of the late and sisters of the present Lord Stanley, of Lathom[5]; and Sir Hugh Venables, of Kinderton, near Middlewich.

All in this list, with the exception of Lord Dudley, were amongst the slain; and it is evident that the gentry of Cheshire were strongly represented. But the force must have been wanting in organisation and cohesion. The units of which it was composed could not have had much opportunity of practising concerted action, so as to gain feelings of mutual reliance. And they had probably seen less actual fighting than their opponents, by reason of the Welsh March being more tranquil than that of Scotland. But we may be quite certain that they were actuated by strong feelings of local patriotism, and of hostility to the Northern marauders, whose presence they resented as an intrusion.

---

4. Brooke, p. 27, where the authorities are given.
5. This appears to be correct; but Ormerod in one (Vol. 2) place says that it was Sir John Troutbeck, father of Sir William, who was killed. Sir William is sometimes described as "of Dunham"; but in the Herald's pedigree of 1589 he is said to be "of Prynes Castle in Wirral."

CHAPTER 5

The Ground

(A) *General Features of Boreheath and its Vicinity.* The character of Audley's army must have influenced him in his selection of the ground on which to fight. He would wish to be in the open, where his superior numbers and his cavalry could be employed to advantage; and to avoid forest fighting, which requires a special training and is always hazardous. He determined, therefore, to take up a position immediately to the South of the great North Staffordshire forest region, so as to intercept his adversary as soon as he emerged from it.

The Southernmost part of Boreheath was the place which he selected for his position; and this was to a great extent open ground, but not by any means entirely so. In 1587 the unenclosed waste of Boreheath amounted to about six hundred acres; and in 1459 it was probably a little more. It belonged to the Manor of Tyrley, which included, besides Tyrley, the townships of Blore, Almington, and Hales.

The hamlet of Blore[1] is at present represented by two farms, which stand on an exposed knoll more than 500 feet above the sea; but was formerly more populous.[2] It stands to the South-east of Boreheath, and was on Audley's right flank.

About half a mile to the South of it is Hales[3]; and a mile to

---

1. Blore is derived from the same root as "blow," "blare," and "blast," and means an exposed and windy place.—Duignan.
2. The pannage list of 1555 gives fourteen householders in Blore.
3. Hales, from "healh," meadow, or pasture. Duignan.

the West of Hales is Almington,[4] the most important of the three villages.

Half a mile to the North of Almington is another small cluster of houses belonging to Almington, known as Sandy Lane. Blore, Hales, Almington, and Sandy Lane form the corners of a quadrilateral, in which were situated the common cornfields of the three villages: that of Blore on the East, that of Almington on the West, and that of Hales in the centre. These fields formed a tract of more or less level country, about a mile long by half a mile wide, joining on to the Southern end of Bloreheath, and sloping gradually to the South and West. They were fenced round while the corn was growing; but after harvest[5] were thrown open, so that the cattle of the tenants might have common of pasture over them.

It must have been a great convenience to Audley to have this open and unencumbered space in rear of his position, on which to pitch his camp,[6] park his baggage train, and exercise his troops. Moreover, the slope of the Almington cornfield towards the South, down to a hollow known as Cromodale, or Crumbuldale (near the new Bloreheath Farm) would allow him to conceal his force from an enemy approaching from the North.[7] This slope is called in the tithe apportionment the "Bent," a word which seems to mean a declivity, as in "Bowers Bent" in Standon parish.

To the North-east and East of Audley's position was the Rounhay, or Rowney, Wood. The word Rounhay, according to Mr. Duignan, means the rough locality; and this Wood is rough

---

4. Pronounced Ammington, but spelt Alkementon in the 13th century. Probably derived from Alkmund.—Duignan.

5. The battle was fought 23rd September.

6. The Chronicler Rapin says that he was encamped.

7. It is not perhaps an important point, but the bill of impeachment describes the battle as having been fought "at Blore in your shire of Stafford, *in the feldes of the same toune* called Bloreheath. Rot. Parl. 38 Hen. VI. 348.

The quadrilateral was all cultivated in 1587, as well as other land outside of it In 1459 parts of it may still have been waste. And these would be at the Northern end of the Hales and Almington fields, and the Southern end of the Blorefield; that is, at the parts most remote from the respective villages.

enough, as all North Staffordshire fox-hunters know. In the six-teenth century it had become sub-divided: the Northern portion (corresponding to the present Rowney Farm of 140 acres) being known as the Little Rowney; and the Southern portion as the "Brandwood," or "Burnt Wood," the middle portion being called the Great Rowney. The Great Rowney and Brandwood extended as far South as the Park Lane, which divided them from the Park; and included the land now known as the "Cold Comfort Farm."

They also overlapped the North-eastern corner of the Park, took in the existing "Burnt Wood Farm," and extended as far as the Northern limit of the "Knowl Wood." Eastwards, these woods, which covered about 700 acres, extended as far as the boundary of Tyrley Manor, and abutted upon the woods of the Bishop of Lichfteld, which formed part of his Manor of Ec-cleshall. The name Burnt Wood, which has superseded the old name of Great Rowney, is doubtless derived from the operations of the ironfounders, charcoal burners, and glass makers, who obtained their fuel from it; whose doings are commemorated in the names "Smith's Rough," "Smithy Breach," "Glasshouse," and "Coalbrook," and whose refuse heaps are still to be found.[8] But in 1459 the destruction had not perhaps gone very far; and the district to the East of the battlefield was for the most part a dense jungle.[9]

The Park, which comes into the story of the battle, must not be confused with Tyrley Old Park, which lay much farther to the West, near Tyrley Castle. Still less must it be confused with Blore Park, belonging to the Bishop of Lichfield: a great enclo-sure more than a mile in diameter, which lay a little more than three miles to the South-east of Bloreheath, and joined up to Chipnall and Cheswardine.

Tyrley New Park was enclosed by the Le Botiler Lords of

8. The Chronicle of Croxden Abbey records, under date 1345: "The wood of Gibbe rydinges, Lindenecliff, and le Newehaye was burnt and sold to Joseph Skachare for 32 *marks* sterling and two and a-half horseloads of iron." This wood had been burnt before in 1290.

9. The first Statute for the protection of woods was passed in 1543.

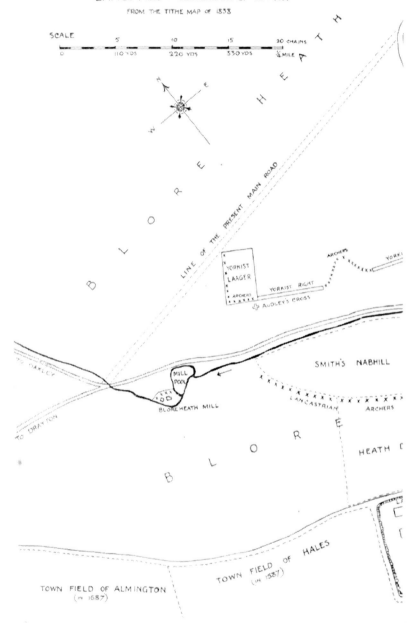

BATTLE-FIELD OF BLOREHEATH 23ᵗʰ SEPT 1459

FROM THE TITHE MAP OF 1833

SCALE

0	5	10	15	20 CHAINS
0	110 YDS	220 YDS	330 YDS	¼ MILE

B L O R E   H E A T H

B L O R E

LINE OF THE PRESENT MAIN ROAD

YORKIST LAAGER

ARCHERS

ARCHERS

YORKI

YORKIST RIGHT

☩ AUDLEY'S CROSS

TO DARLEY

MILL POOL

BLOREHEATH MILL

TO DRAYTON

SMITH'S NABHILL

LANCASTRIAN   ARCHERS

B   L   O   R   E

HEATH

TOWN FIELD OF HALES
(IN 1587)

TOWN FIELD OF ALMINGTON
(IN 1587)

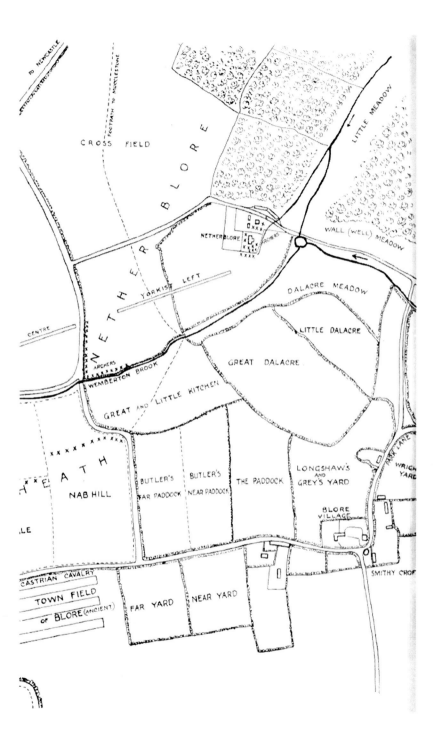

TO NEWCASTLE

FOOTPATH TO MIDDLESTONE

CROSS FIELD

LITTLE MEADOW

N E T H E R   B L O R E

NETHERBLORE

WALL (WELL) MEADOW

YORKIST LEFT

DALACRE MEADOW

CENTRE

LITTLE DALACRE

ARCHERS

GREAT DALACRE

WEMBERTON BROOK

GREAT AND LITTLE KITCHEN

H E A T H

NAB HILL

BUTLER'S
FAR PADDOCK

BUTLER'S
NEAR PADDOCK

THE PADDOCK

LONGSHAW'S
AND
GREY'S YARD

PAW LANE

WRIGHT'S
YARD

BLORE
VILLAGE

LE

CASTRIAN CAVALRY

TOWN FIELD
OF BLORE (ANCIENT)

FAR YARD

NEAR YARD

SMITHY CROFT

Wem and Tyrley in the reign of Edward I., or Edward II.[10]; and was used by them as a hunting ground in the 14th century.[11] In the 15th century the absentee Neville Lords must have let the grazing rights to tenants; and in the 16th century we find the Park divided up. Originally, it must have included about 375 acres, and extended from the Park Lane on the North-east to the Lloyd on the South-west. On the East it was bounded by the Burnt Wood and Knowl Wood, on the South by the Knowl Wood and on the West by the enclosed lands of Blore and Hales. It was divided up as follows, and the division had taken place before 1524:—

	Acres.
1. The Park Spring Wood, including the present Park Spring Farm	191
2. The South-western portion (including the Lloyd Drumble), let with Almington Farm, and called the New Park in 1524. (This portion included a field called the "Chapel Field.")	100
3. The North-western angle, including the fields called Park Field, Park Meadow, Gorsey Hill, the Upper and Lower Pools, and Upper and Lower Furlongs, all of which are, and have long been, held with one of the Blore Farms	84

Audley might have felt quite easy about his right flank, for it was most unlikely that the enemy would enter upon such rough and broken country to try to turn it.

It was also improbable that they would try to work round his left. Had they done so, they would first of all have had to cross the Wemberton Brook, which is an awkward obstacle anywhere. And, had they succeeded in doing that, they would have been liable to be attacked in a most dangerous position between the

10. See the Close Roll of 10 Edward II. (1316).
11. Some men were proceeded against for poaching in this Park in 15 Edward III. Salt Collections, Vol. XIV. 55.

Brook and the River Tern, where defeat would have meant annihilation.

(B) *The Actual Battlefield.* We have now to consider more particularly the ground which Audley occupied and had in front of him, that which lies to the North and West of the hamlet of Blore. From the cornfield the ground slopes gradually down to a little brook, which runs East and West, and has a narrow valley with steep banks. On the modern, large-scale ordnance maps it is called the "Hemp-mill Brook"; and this was the name by which Mr. Brooke knew it in 1853. But in 1554[12] it was known as the "Wemberton Brook"; and in a Charter of the 13th century it is called "Wambrimbroc."[13]

The meaning of this latter name is easy to understand. Warn, or Wem, is from the same Anglo-Saxon root as womb, and means a hollow; brim means border, or bank. So that the ancient name signifies "The brook with the hollowed-out channel." This brook is formed by several small streamlets flowing from the North-east, East, and South-east, which meet near the place marked on the ordnance map as "Blore Farm"; and close to this farm is a strong spring, formerly known as Blore Wall,[14] the water from which also flows into the brook. Below the farm the brook runs for the most part between steep banks for the rest of its course, some two miles, till it joins the river Tern between Oakley and Tunstall.

In order to realise the problem which was engaging Audley's attention, it is necessary to understand what the roads were like in his time. They were very different from what they are now; and it must suffice here to state the writer's conclusions on the subject, reserving arguments and proofs for separate consideration in Appendix C.

The straight wide and well-graded road which now crosses Bloreheath, running nearly East and West, did not then exist.

---

12. Tyrley Court Roll.
13. Charter of Sir William le Botiler to the Abbey of Cumbermere.—Tunstall papers.
14. "Wall "means well or spring. To wall means to boil; as salt walling = salt boiling.

It is the result of a Turnpike Act, and an Inclosure Act, passed in 1768 and 1773 respectively. Before that time travellers proceeding from Newcastle to Market Drayton, and entering Tyrley Manor where the Loggerheads Inn now stands, would follow the line of the present road past the Rowney Farm and the Folly Plantation. But about a hundred yards beyond the plantation the old road bent considerably to the left, and followed the course of the present bridle road from Mucclestone to Blore as far as the Wemberton Brook. From this point the road to Blore village, steep, crooked, and worn into a deep hollow by the traffic of ages and the action of water, crossed the brook and led more or less straight on in a Southerly direction.

But persons going to Drayton would here turn to the right and proceed Westwards along the valley of the Wemberton Brook, passing between Audley Cross and the old Bloreheath cornmill. So that for a distance of about 750 yards the road passed through a narrow defile (coming out again on to the open heath ground on the Southern side of the valley, after passing the mill pond), and proceeded much as at present to Sandy Lane and Shifford's Bridge. Here then was the "pass" mentioned by the chronicler Rapin, which has given such trouble to commentators, more especially Mr. Snape. And it was the existence of this defile, and the determination to contest the passage of it, which caused Audley to take up the position he did.

With regard to other roads then existing, it is likely that the road along the Wemberton Brook valley was not confined to the above-mentioned 750 yards, but extended up the valley into the woodlands and ultimately to Eccleshall, and also downstream to the Tern at Oakley Mill. The road from Sandy Lane to Mucclestone went as it does now, crossing the Wemberton Brook, by a ford with deep and narrow approaches, near to the existing bridge. And there was a track leading from Blore village to Sandy Lane, skirting the Northern edge of the common cornfields and running parallel to Audley's line of front. But the road which now crosses the main road at right-angles below Bloreheath mill, and leads to Hales and Blore in one direction and to Mucclestone in the other, is modern, and was made after the Inclosure Act.

As regards the other features of the ground, the pond called Daisy Lake, which lies in the valley below Bloreheath mill, does not seem to be older than the end of the 17th or beginning of the 18th century.[15] The banks of the valley were probably originally a good deal steeper than they are at present. Road-making, gravel digging, irrigation, ploughing, and rabbits have all had a tendency to tone them down and wear away their sharpness; but that in their natural state they offered a considerable obstacle is evidenced by the twisting of the road in order to avoid them.

It is likely that Audley's left flank rested on the mill, and that he did not occupy any of the ground beyond it, though he would, of course, keep it under observation. As already pointed out, it would be easy for him to frustrate any attempt of the enemy to pass on this side of him. The mill is undoubtedly ancient, and is mentioned in the 14th century "Extents" of the Manor.[16] The mill house still remains, but the mill is gone and the pond is dry. Both were there, however, in 1838, when the tithe map was made. When the water was pounded up, the brook above the mill must have been a more serious obstacle than it is at present.

Turning to Audley's right flank, we see on the maps that in front of it lies the homestead at present known as Blore Farm. This is a place of great antiquity, being a freehold carved out of the Manor of Tyrley by William Pantulf who died in 1233. This information comes from the Chartulary at Oakley, which was compiled about the year 1720. At that date there was in existence a Charter by which the aforesaid William Pantulf granted to John Mevrell of Bluer a hide of land[17] in the vill of Bluer, the boundaries of which were given Most unfortunately this deed has long been missing, and the information which it contained

---

15. I have not found it mentioned earlier than 1704. In 1711 a fulling mill stood between it and the lane, to which it furnished the water power. The watercourse from it to Shifford's Grange dates from early in the 19th century.—Tunstall papers.

16. Pub. Record Office. P.M. Inquests of the le Botilers.

17. About 180 acres, according to Fleta, who wrote in the time of Edward I.

has been lost.

The presumption nevertheless is that the boundaries of this land, like those of the granges granted by the Pantulfs to the monks at Combermere, were formed either by streams or ancient tracks; and that the Northern and Western sides of this "hide of land in the vill of Bluer" were bounded in the 13th century by the road leading from Newcastle to Market Drayton, as we know that they were in Queen Elizabeth's reign.[18]

Another Charter relating to this place dates from 1339, and by it Hugo Cabot de Buntanesdale granted to Hugo de Hulle his capital messuage, with the adjacent land and meadows in the vill of Netherblore, together with his bondman (*nativus*) Thomas Godfre, and all his family (*sequela*), and all his goods and chattels; and with the homage and services of William, the son of Thomas, the shepherd, and of his other tenants in the same vill of Netherblore. This Hugo de Hulle, or Hill, took his name from the Titterstone Clee Hill, near Ludlow, and was the ancestor of the Hills, of Hawkstone.[19] His son William Hill married the heiress of Buntingsdale, and died in 1371, leaving a son Griffin Hill who lived till 1434. Humphrey Hill, the son of the latter, appears to have held these lands till 1484. And in 1515 his son William died in possession of them. This William was born about 1444, and lived at Netherblore in his father's lifetime[20], but hardly so early as 1459.

This capital messuage of Netherblore was therefore a place of some importance; it was probably moated and capable of defence; and with its fences and inclosures had an important bearing upon the battle. When Audley was on the defensive, he would depend upon it to protect his right flank; and when he became the assailant, it prevented him from getting at the Yorkist left, and compelled him to attack their centre and right. In 1773[21] the

18. The map of 1773, at Oakley, shows this farm surrounded by roads, except where it is joined up to the Burnt Wood and Rowney.
19. Herald's Visitation of Shropshire, 1623.
20. Close Roll of 1472.
21. A survey of the farm was made at this date, and a map drawn, which is now at Oakley.

farm contained 190 acres; and there is no reason to suppose that its original boundaries had been in any way altered.

About twenty acres of it, known as the Dalacre, or Dallacre,[22] lie to the South of the brook. It is good land, and probably formed part of the original arable land of the farm, and was fenced round at a very early date. And beyond it, on the East, lay boggy meadows bordering on the forest. I think it probable that all the land lying between the Dalacre, the cornfield of Blore, and the old lane leading down to the defile was already enclosed in 1459. It is all of good quality, it lies close to the village; and for a considerable part of its total length the ditch of the boundary fence of the Dalacre is on the inside and not on the outside, which suggests that some of the adjoining land was inclosed earlier even than the Dalacre itself.[23]

It is probable that the entire farm of Netherblore, being held in severalty, and lying in a ring fence, was hedged round in 1459. But as to this we cannot be absolutely certain. The Abbot of Combermere held Stafford's Grange in the same way, and had the right to take fencing materials from the Tyrley woods: yet a considerable portion of the poorer land of this grange remained open waste so late as 1773.

The question as to whether the land on the South side of the defile and on the West side of the old lane was inclosed or not, is more difficult to decide. We know from the Writ of Partition that there was uninclosed waste lying between the Bloreheath mill pool and the village cornfields in 1587. It was computed to amount to 36 acres, but was probably rather more, perhaps 40 or 45. But, after allowing for this, there still remains a piece of about 24 acres; which at the time of the Tithe Survey was divided into three fields, known as Nab Hill, Smith's Nab Hill, and Heath Dale.

---

22. Probably from Dale or Dell, as this ground lies in the valley.
23. Three of these fields are known as "The Paddock" and "Butler's far and near Paddocks." This seems to put these inclosures back to the time of the Butler, or le Botiler, lords of Tyrley; the last of whom died in 1369. The fields between the Paddocks and .the brook are called the "Great and Little Kitchen," and contain 7¼ acres. Possibly they may have been the common vegetable plot of the village.

This was evidently inclosed land in 1587, and let with one of the Blore farms; the question is whether it was inclosed in 1459 or not. Nab, or Knob, is no doubt derived from a little hillock in the Nab Hill field; and it does not suggest anything as to the date of inclosure, nor does Heath Dale. But the name of Smith throws a ray of light. Andrew Smith occupied a large farm at Blore, and also the Bloreheath mill, in 1587; and it is very likely that he was the man who inclosed this tongue of land, which runs down to the mill. I do not find the name of Smith in connection with Blore before this date, though there were men of that name at the "Walk Mill," near Market Drayton, fifty years earlier, and at Almington in 1439.[24] The inference, therefore, seems to be that Smith's Nab Hill, at any rate, and probably the other two fields also, would be open heath ground at the time of the battle.

These doubtful fences are shown upon the map with dotted lines. If they were in existence, and were lined by Lancastrians on the morning of the day, they would have added to the difficulty of the Yorkists in forcing a passage through the defile. But they would also have made it difficult for the Lancastrian horse to range themselves in front of the Yorkist line of battle, as Waurin says they did; and would have greatly hindered their cavalry charges. On the whole, I should be inclined to guess that none of these fences were then in existence; but were made between 1459 and 1587. Inclosure was proceeding at that time, we know; for the Court Roll of 1556 refers to "the newly-enclosed land at Crumbuldale field." At any rate it is quite clear that there was no fence along the Northern bank of the defile.

The woodland certainly came very near to the Netherblore homestead on the Eastern side; for, besides the Great Rowney Wood which bounded the property, a large proportion of the little domain itself was still timbered. Even in 1773 ten acres remained so, and the field names, "Burnt Wood Field" and "New Hay," which refer to another twenty-three acres, are suggestive of clearings. And the post mortem inquest of Richard Wilbraham (who died possessed of this farm in 1612) states that more

---

24. Old papers at Tunstall.

than a quarter of it was still uncleared in the reign of James I.[25] The land on this side of the farm is all strong clay, and grows good oak trees at the present day.

It is evident therefore that Audley occupied a defensive position of great strength; and that on general grounds he could afford to bide his time and await developments. We have now to enquire into the question of the arms and tactics of the period; and we shall see that there were strong additional reasons which made it imperative for him to play a waiting game.

---

25. The descriptions of the farm are rather difficult to reconcile. The Inquests p.m. of the Hill family, dated 1371, 1434, and 1515, give no information. A fine levied in 1601 gives the parcels as "a messuage and garden, 100 acres of arable, 20 of meadow, 60 of pasture, 10 of wood, and 200 of furze and heath total 390." The Inquest p.m. of Richard Wilbraham, taken in 1612, gives the quantities as 20 acres arable, 15 of meadow, 20 of pasture, 20 of wood total 75. As to the first estimate, the parcels in fines have no pretensions to accuracy, and are made all-embracing. The post mortem verdicts on the other hand usually understate land values. Besides which the Wilbrahams were in the habit of using the Cheshire acre; which was measured with an eight yard rod, instead of with one of five and a-half, and contained more than two statute acres. There was also a local acre in use in Blore, called the Bloreland acre.

CHAPTER 6

Arms, Tactics, and Generalship

(A) *Arms and Tactics*. It has already been said that the Yorkists had no artillery,[1] and do not appear to have made any serious use of gunpowder; and the same remark applies to the Lancastrians. Both armies were of the old-fashioned type, relying upon the long bow as their missile weapon, and upon pikemen and billmen and armoured horsemen for fighting at close quarters. Weapons of war were much what they had been in the reign of Edward III.; the only difference being that the armour now worn was thicker and heavier, to afford more complete protection against arrows. This of course added to the weight that men and horses had to carry, and greatly impeded all offensive movements.

Moreover, though the horses had now bards on their heads and breasts, they were still without protection from flank attack; wounded horses were worse than useless, for they made confusion worse confounded, and mounted cavalry were at a great disadvantage against archers posted behind cover. For these reasons, and as the result of experience gained in the Scotch and French wars, it had become customary for armies to act upon the defensive whenever possible; and also for knights and men-at-arms to fight on foot. Time after time victories had been won by adopting a crescent-shaped formation; the recessed centre formed of pikemen, assisted by dismounted cavalry and knights;

---

1. The Yorkists used guns at St. Albans in 1455; and at this time they had them at Ludlow. Rot. Parl. 38 Hen. VI. Vol. V. 347-8.

51

and the advanced horns composed of archers, concealed or posted behind obstacles. The heavily armed men were able to arrest
the onslaught of the enemy, and the archers took advantage of
this to gall their flanks and rear with flights of arrows.

Against the Scots these tactics had succeeded at Dupplin
Moor in 1332 (which was what the lawyers call the "leading
case"), at Halidon Hill in 1333, at Neville's Cross in 1346, and at
Homildon Hill in 1402. The French had given way before them
at Crecy in 1346, and at Poictiers in 1356; and the Spaniards,
to whom they were still a novelty, at Navarette in 1357, and at
Aljubarotta in 1385.[2] The only way to meet them successfully
was by resolutely refusing to attack.

We should have expected that Audley, bearing these consid-
erations in mind, would have dismounted most of his horsemen,
and taken up a defensive position on the rising ground to the
South of the defile, posting archers on his right flank opposite
to Netherblore, and also in the curtilage of Bloreheath mill, and
a third body of them in the centre to guard the lane that crosses
the valley; and that he would have kept a mounted reserve to
frustrate any unlooked-for move on the part of the enemy, and
to make a counter attack, or take up the pursuit, in the event of
his defence proving successful. But we are not told that he did
anything of the kind; he seems to have only thought of carrying
out the orders of his Royal mistress in the spirit in which they
were given, and of riding down and capturing his opponents.

Waurin, whose information came from a Yorkist source, says
that at daybreak Salisbury and his men could see their adversaries behind a great overgrown hedge, with only the tips of their
pennons showing above it. From which it would appear that
the Yorkists, on emerging from the Rowney Wood on to Bloreheath, looked across the defile (which would be hidden from
their view) to the rising ground beyond it; and there saw their
enemies screened by the hedge of the village cornfields. Waurin
also tells us of the overweening confidence of Audley's men, and

2. See *The History of the Art of War in the Middle Ages*, by Professor C. W. Oman, a
work to which the present writer is greatly indebted.

how cheaply they held their foes.

(B) *Salisbury's Defensive Measures.* Salisbury and his army, on the other hand, were actuated rather by the patient and phlegmatic temperament of their chief, the Duke of York. They did not act rashly, but with prudence and resolution; and in their arrangements displayed much of the wisdom of the serpent. Being greatly outnumbered, they felt no strong confidence in the result; but determined to sell their lives dearly, and to adopt the defensive tactics which experience had shown to be the best. Halting on the North side of the defile, under the shelter of the Rowney Wood, they dismounted and proceeded to fortify a position. In their front was the slope, with the brook at the bottom of it; and on their left this afforded very complete protection, not only because the brook banks were steep, but also on account of the fences and ditches surrounding the mansion and lands of Netherblore; their flank resting upon the wood.

Opposite to their centre and left there seem to have been no artificial obstacles, but only the slope and brook. In places the slope was steep, almost precipitous; but in others it was more gradual, and at some distance from the brook, which ran between low banks. And their right was very weak, being unprotected and entirely "in the air." This part therefore received special attention, as we learn from Waurin; a laager of carts and horses all fastened together was formed, stakes were driven into the ground to protect their front, and their rear was secured by an intrenchment. It is probable that the right flank of the Yorkists was opposite to Bloreheath mill, but out of bowshot from it, and a little to the West of Audley's Cross.

The length of front which they had to cover was something over half a mile, and their force would give them about five men to each yard of ground. It is likely that the knights and men-at-arms would be posted in the centre, where the ground was more flat, and where a lane crossed the defile. They would of course be assisted by archers on their flanks and wherever cover could be had or the ground was favourable. The left of the position, being less vulnerable, would require fewer men; but the right, being weak, would want every one that could be spared. We may suppose that the line was divided into three sections, each under its own commander, and each composed partly of spearmen and partly of archers. Having completed their preparations, we are told that they prostrated themselves on the ground, and worshipped in the most humble and devout manner.

CHAPTER 7

The Fighting

(A) *Salisbury's Stratagem*. Salisbury had some reason to fear
that the assault would not be made, or at any rate pressed home;
in short that the Lancastrians might adopt the course which
in recent years had been always taken by the French in such
cases, and decline to fight. Situated as he was in a hostile country, outnumbered, and expecting to be hemmed in by other
forces which the Queen was assembling, fearing also that supplies might fail, he could not afford to wait indefinitely. He had
to persuade his enemies to throw aside caution, and make an
attack, which the Lancastrians on their part were ready enough
to do.

With this object in view, Salisbury pretended to retreat in
confusion. This movement was probably confined to his centre,
and did not extend to his intrenched flanks; and it did not proceed very far. His pikemen retired just far enough to encourage
their opponents to come down into the defile, where they had
rising ground in front of them and the Yorkist archers on their
flanks,[1] as well as in front of them. As soon as the Lancastrians
were seen to be fairly committed to the attack and charging
down into the valley, the Yorkists halted, turned about, and prepared to hold their ground, probably returning to their original
position on the brink of the declivity as being the most advanta-
geous for them.

---

1. The same trick was practised by the Yorkists at the Battle of Tewkesbury.

(B) *Lancastrian Cavalry Charges.* Waurin says that the battle began with a furious discharge of arrows on both sides, under cover of which Audley's[2] men attacked on horseback. The arrows killed about 20 Yorkists, and many of the horses in the laager, who probably acted as a screen to the men near them. But the Lancastrians, being in the open and unprotected, suffered much heavier loss, five or six hundred men falling before they drew off out of range. They soon however returned to the charge; but were again repulsed with a loss of a hundred men, while they only killed ten Yorkists in return.

(C) *Death of Audley.* It would seem that in this second cavalry charge Audley was killed. Tradition says that the man who killed him was Sir Roger Kynaston of Stocks near Ellesmere, a leading Shropshire Yorkist; and that to commemorate the event he added Audley's coat of arms to his own.[3]

(D) *Change of Command.* Lord Dudley s Tactics. The command then devolved upon Lord Dudley (misdescribed by Waurin as the Seigneur de Beaumont[4]), who determined to dismount his cavalry, to the number of four thousand or so, and attack on foot. Then ensued a hand to hand tussle which lasted more than half an hour; the remainder of the Lancastrian horsemen remaining mounted and giving no assistance.

And, upon the attack failing, a body of them numbering five hundred joined the enemy and began attacking their own side. This was the final disaster, the Lancastrian resistance collapsed, and the Yorkists had only to advance to complete the rout. Gregory says that the battle lasted all the afternoon, from one o'clock till five, and that the pursuit was continued till "seven at the bell in the morning."

(E) *The Defeat and Losses.* The loss of the Lancastrians is es-

---

2. Waurin calls the Lancastrian Commander the Duke of Exeter. He also says that Warwick was with his father. Of course neither of them were present. Exeter, though a strong Lancastrian, had married the Duke of York's sister.
3. Sir Roger was certainly with the Duke at Ludlow a few weeks later. Blakeway's *Sheriffs of Shropshire.*
4. John Viscount Beaumont was killed at Northampton in 1460.

timated at two thousand four hundred dead,[5] and that of the Yorkists at fifty-six.[6] The heavily-armoured knights and esquires always had a difficulty in escaping after a reverse, especially when righting dismounted; and that was certainly so on the present occasion. The flower of Audley's army was either slain or captured on the field itself. Among the prisoners were Lord Dudley, who was wounded, Sir Thomas Fitton, and a dozen[7] other knights; but their names are not recorded.

(F) *The Pursuit.* The flight of the vanquished would probably be towards Market Drayton, and would be hampered by the river Tern. In summer this might be crossed at various places, but the most convenient spot would be at Stafford's (or Sheep-ford) Bridge. There is little doubt that there was a bridge here in 1459, as there certainly was in 1476,[8] built by the Abbot of Combermere to give him ready access to his two Granges, Shifford's and Broomhall. Two of the fields on Shifford's Grange, near the river, have peculiar names one is called Deadman's Den. and the other Duke Langley's piece. But whether they are in any way connected with the battle, I am unable to say.

(G) Audleys Burial. Audley's burial took place at Darley Abbey, close to his Derbyshire Manor house of Markeaton: a monastery of which his Touchet ancestors had been benefactors so early as the reign of Henry II. And there can be little doubt that the other dead knights were honourably interred by their friends. Insults to the dead had not yet become customary.[9]

(H) *Reflections on the Battle.* It is, of course, easy to be wise after the event, and to say what ought to have been done by people who are dead and can make no reply. But it does seem

---

5. This is the figure usually given. Waurin says about two thousand.
6. This is Waurin's estimate, the only one that I have seen.
7. According to Waurin.
8. A deed of that date, at Tunstall, mentions "*pons de Shyfford.*" It was a narrow horse-bridge, and was replaced by the present bridge about 1768.
9. The Duke of York's head was exposed, after his death, with a paper crown on it, in 1460. The body of Richard III. was stripped naked and tied to a horse, and so shown, after Bosworth, in 1485.

reasonably certain that, had Audley managed his attack better, the result of the battle would have been very different. A portion of his large force might have made a demonstration in front of the Yorkists, engaging their attention, and preventing them from moving; while the remainder, keeping to the lower part of the heath and following the lane leading to Mucclestone, might have crossed the Wemberton Brook and worked round their exposed right flank. A charge upon their rear, which might have been delivered with great impetus down the sloping ground, would have brushed away any such slight obstacles as they could have made in the time and with the materials at their disposal; their right would have been crushed, and their whole line rolled up and destroyed.

CHAPTER 8

Dangerous Situation of the Victors

(A) *Yorkists Exhausted and Scattered.* After the battle the victors had little time to trouble about the vanquished, and were fully occupied with their own concerns. And indeed their position was a critical one, as is testified by the Chronicler Gregory. Had the Queen been able to send a comparatively small force of fresh troops from Eccleshall, to march through the woodlands and take them suddenly in rear, the result must have been disastrous to them. Exhausted as they were after their hard day, many of them scattered far and wide in the pursuit, and the remainder encumbered with prisoners and wounded, they could not have offered a very effective resistance. We know too that there was a force of two thousand men in a position to make such an attack, if its commander had been so minded.

(B) *Doubtful Attitude of Lord Stanley.* This army was under Thomas Lord Stanley, who had great estates in Lancashire and Cheshire.[1] We learn from the Bill of Impeachment that he had sent his servant to the Queen, promising to come in haste, and asking to be put in the forefront of the battle. But he did not keep his word, and remained for three days inactive at Newcastle. He also sent his brother William[2] to join Salisbury before the battle, and wrote him a letter of congratulation after it. This is not at all surprising when we remember that Salisbury was his

---

1. In Lancashire he had Lathom, and Liverpool; in Cheshire he had Bidston, Neston, and Dunham Massey.
2. William had Holt Castle in Denbighshire, and Ridley in Cheshire.

father-in-law; but he wavered between his duty to his Sovereign and his private feelings, and does not seem to have been a man upon whom it was safe to rely.[3]

(C) *The Forward Movement Covered by Another Ruse.* His situation being such, Salisbury had every reason for pressing forward. He would wish first to follow up his beaten foes and prevent them from rallying; secondly, to reach Market Drayton and obtain supplies and succour for his wounded; and thirdly, to exchange his precarious position for a more secure one. Gregory says that he covered his evacuation of Bloreheath by a clever ruse, deputing an Austin friar to shoot guns all night "in the Park that was at the back side of the field"; and that in the morning nobody was found in the Park except the friar.

(D) *The Chapel and the Friar.* With regard to the friar and the Park, a curious point may be noted. It is well-known that there was a chapel, or oratory, in Tyrley, which is mentioned in the Bishop's register so early as 1361; and was still in existence in 1562, as is proved by the Court Rolls of the Manor. There was also a chapelry tithe connected with it, which still existed when the Tithe Commutation Act was passed. But all memory of the site of this chapel has passed away. In the middle of this quondam Park there is, however, a field which bears the name of the "Chapel Field"; and in this field is an excrescence which seems to mark the site of an ancient building, which is not accounted for in any of the existing maps, one of which goes back to 1669. It seems quite a natural inference that Tyrley Chapel stood here, and that its guardian was the Austin friar who fired alarm guns on the night of St. Tecla's Day.

In those early days, when gunpowder was still something of a novelty, the firing of blank charges would have a more alarming effect than it would now. And the plan seems to have answered; for Salisbury was able to collect his scattered and wearied men, and transport them to a better position without any molestation.

3. Lord Stanley was only 26 years old at this time. His father had recently died, so that he had only lately succeeded to his responsibilities, and had not had much experience.

CHAPTER 9

Salisbury Hill

(A) *Salisbury's Camp*. It is likely that, after the battle, the tenants of Tyrley Manor came to pay their respects to the uncle of their landlord, asked his protection, and placed their local knowledge at his disposal. And it is evident that the camping ground on Salisbury Hill was selected by someone who knew the district; for it would have been difficult to find a better one. The hill has a flat top, large enough to provide space for several thousand men; and from it the ground slopes in every direction, so that the camp would not be easily rushed. At present there are a good many trees on it and round it; but in the 15th century it was bare heath, and stood in the middle of an open country, so that the view from it was extensive and uninterrupted. It was well supplied with water, having a spring near its summit, in addition to the River Tern winding round its base.

It was near to the town of Drayton, with which it was probably connected by a bridge.[1] But it lay on the South-west side of the town, with open country behind it, so that its occupants could easily slip away towards Ludlow whenever they desired. This they would wish to do, and probably did, as soon as possible. The Bill of Impeachment tells us that Salisbury was at Drayton on the night after the battle, and also on the Monday morning; and that he knew that Lord Stanley was not coming to join him. There was, therefore, nothing to detain him; and

---

1. There was a stone horse-bridge over the Tern at Walk-mill just below Salisbury Hill. A will of 1553 has a bequest of money to repair it: so it may well have been there in 1459.

61

we may assume that, having despatched his two wounded sons northwards, attended to his other injured men, and taken what supplies he could get, he pushed on towards Ludlow some time on Monday.

(B) *His March to Ludlow*. What route he took does not seem to be recorded. He may have crossed the Severn at Shrewsbury, where the Duke of York was very popular, and where the bridge had been recently repaired.[2] or he may have left the Wrekin on his right hand, and proceeded by Newport, Shifnal, Bridgnorth, and Cleobury Mortimer.

---

2. *Shrewsbury*, by Thomas Auden (1906).

Chapter 10

Queen Margaret at Mucclestone

Queen Margaret on Mucclestone Church Tower. There is a local tradition that Queen Margaret rode from Eccleshall to the scene of conflict, and was an eye-witness of the battle; that she viewed it from the tower of Mucclestone Church; that when the day was lost she fled, having first had her horse's shoes reversed so as to mislead any pursuers; and that the blacksmith who did this for her was named Skelhorn.[1] At first sight this seems a most unlikely story. Mucclestone Church is a mile and a-half from the field of battle, which is now completely hidden from it by a plantation called the "Folly." To get to it from Eccleshall, the Queen would have had to cross the line of Salisbury's advance; and supposing her to have reached it in safety, she would have been in rear of his army. In case the Yorkists had been driven back, they might have retired by way of Mucclestone, cutting her off from Eccleshall, and very possibly making her a prisoner.

But to these objections it may be answered, first, that the plantation is comparatively modern, and that in 1459 the ground on which it stands was open heath; so that part, at any rate, of the battlefield would at that time be visible from the tower. Secondly, that it might have been possible, though perhaps risky, to pass in rear of the Yorkist army after it had established itself in its entrenchments and was awaiting attack. Thirdly, that (as we are told by Waurin), the Lancastrians expected to capture their

---

1. Hinchliffe's *History of Barthomley*. Skelhorn's lineal descendant was blacksmith and parish clerk at Mucclestone in 1855.

adversaries with very little trouble and loss to themselves; so that the risk may not have appeared to them at the time to be very great. It may be, also, that the Queen was expecting further help from her friends in Cheshire, and thought that she was quite safe in advancing in that direction.

As to what became of her after the defeat of her army, accounts differ. Leland says that she returned to Eccleshall, where she remained under the protection of John Hales, the Bishop of Lichfield and Lord of Eccleshall Castle. But Canon Morris, a later authority, states that whilst flying from the field to Chester she was captured by John Cleger, one of Lord Stanley's servants, and spoiled of her jewels; and that whilst her baggage was being rifled she and her son escaped, and succeeded in reaching Harlech Castle.[2] Canon Morris does not give his authority for this story. If it is true, the action of John Cleger is significant as to Lord Stanley's leanings.

2. *History of Chester.*

CHAPTER 11

Events After the Battle

(A) *The Rout of Ludford.* The subsequent adventures of the principal combatants can soon be related. Salisbury effected his intended junction with York and Warwick at Ludlow: but they remained inactive at their camp at Ludford, while the King's army rapidly increased. And soon their followers became demoralised, and obeyed the Royal proclamation to disperse. This scattering of the Yorkist forces was known as the "Rout of Ludford," and occurred on 13th October. For the time being the cause was lost, and the leaders had to seek safety in flight. York escaped to Ireland, where he had friends. Salisbury and Warwick with young Edward Earl of March, after many adventures and a hazardous voyage round Land's End, found refuge at Calais, where they arrived just in the nick of time.

(B) *The New Lord Audley Turns Yorkist.* Not only did they prevent Calais from falling into the hands of their enemies, but they took captive Lord Audley's son and successor, who was with the beseiging force. Strange as it may seem, this Lord Audley forgave the Nevilles for the death of his father and the slight that they had put upon his mother, and became a devoted adherent of the cause of York.

(C) *Salisbury's Death.* Salisbury, was not with the army that won the battle of Northampton in July 1460, having been left behind to besiege the Tower of London, and to secure the support of the city for the Yorkist cause. But in the following December he was wounded and captured at the battle of Wakefield, and afterwards beheaded. His remains subsequently received honourable burial at Bisham Abbey, near Marlow. After his death his Yorkshire estates were plundered by his Lancastrian nephews, Ralph, Earl of Westmorland, and Thomas, his brother.

(D) *Adventures of His Two Sons, John and Thomas*. Salisbury's two sons Sir John and Sir Thomas Neville were wounded at Bloreheath, but were able to proceed northwards, with their brother-in-law Sir Thomas Harrington, the day after the battle. But at Tarporley they were captured by young John Done (a youth of 17, whose father Sir John had been killed in the battle), and committed prisoners to Chester Castle. There they remained till 13th July following, when in obedience to the King's order they were handed over to Lord Stanley. The battle of Northampton had been fought on 9th July, and the King was a prisoner and a puppet in the hands of the Yorkists.[1] Thomas, like his father, lost his life at Wakefield; and John was killed with his brother Warwick at Barnet in 1471. Harrington was slain at Wakefield.

(E) The Stanleys. After the campaign of Bloreheath, the two Stanleys may be assumed to have given a general support to the Yorkist cause, though they did not become prominent during the next quarter of a century.[2] But in 1485 they were again obliged to make a difficult choice, and to decide whether to side with Richard or Henry at the battle of Bosworth. Richard thought that he could count upon them, he having bestowed many favours upon Lord Stanley; and by way of additional security having detained his son, George Lord Strange as a hostage. And, at the beginning of the battle, both the Stanleys, with their united following of eight thousand men, were ranged on his side.

But in the middle of the conflict they deserted him and

---

1. This appears to be the true account. *Vide* Gregory's Chronicle and Canon Morris' *History of Chester*. Mr. Brooke's account, founded on Hall, Hollinshed, Baker, and Stow, differs somewhat.
2. In 1459 Thomas the elder brother was only 26 years old.

joined Henry, whose victory was thereby assured. And it was Lord Stanley who proclaimed Henry King. What motives influenced them does not seem to be quite certain. Their action may have been taken entirely on public grounds, and from detestation of Richard's conduct. But it must not be forgotten that Lord Stanley was, and had been for many years,[3] the stepfather of Henry, whose mother had married him as her third husband. So that it is equally likely that private feeling had something to do with it; and that the influence of his living wife proved stronger than his attachment to the relations of his former one. For his services at Bosworth Lord Stanley was created Earl of Derby, and he died a natural death in 1504.

William, the younger brother, who was knighted about 1465, was not so fortunate. After the battle of Bosworth he had possessed himself of Richard's treasure chest, and by so doing became the richest subject in the land. He lived at Holt Castle, in Denbighshire, and had a roll of "old rents"[4] amounting to 3,000 a year. He had also 40,000 *marks* of ready money. He aspired to become Earl of Chester, which annoyed King Henry, who also had his eye on Stanley's wealth. In 1495 a charge of disloyalty was brought against him; and though it was not supported by much evidence, he was brought to the block and all his property confiscated.[5]

(F) Lord Dudley. Turning now to the Lancastrians, Lord Dudley, who was wounded and captured, may be assumed to have recovered his liberty after the Rout of Ludford. He received several honourable offices from King Henry, and was made a Knight of the Garter. After the accession of Edward IV. in 1461, he received a pardon and grants of money, and was still actively employed in 1478.[6] He died in 1482.[7]

---

3. Lord Stanley was already married to the Countess of Richmond in the year 1473. Rot. Parl. 13 Ed. IV.Vol.VI. 77.

4. "Old rents "were fixed early in the 14th century; and would be much below the real value at the end of the 15th.

5. Ormerod's *Cheshire*,Vol. II.

6. Ormerod,Vol. II.

7. Harwood's edition of *Erdeswick's Staffordshire*.

(G) *Sir Thomas Fitton and Others*. He and Sir Thomas Fitton[8] seem to have been the only survivors of eminence on this side, the names of the other prisoners not having been recorded. Earwaker, in his history of East Cheshire, gives a list of Sir Thomas Fitton's contingent. They numbered sixty-six in all, of whom no less than thirty-one were killed.

8. Of Gawsworth, near Macclesfield.

CHAPTER 12

Was the Battle Fratricidal?

Great stress has been laid by some writers upon the fratricidal character of this battle. Michael Drayton, in his *Polyolbion*, song 22 (which was written in the reign of James I., about 170 years after the battle) says that Dutton fought against Dutton, Done against Done, Booth against Booth, Leigh against Leigh, Venables against Venables, Troutbeck against Troutbeck, Molineux against Molineux, and Egerton against Egerton. And he adds:—

O! Cheshire, wer't thou mad, of thine own native gore
So much until this day thou never shed'st before.

On the other hand, Mr. Beamont, writing in 1850, says that this is a poetic fable, and that all the Cheshire men died fighting in the Queen's livery of the Silver Swan.

It may be worthwhile to consider whether there is any truth in Drayton's charge, which is certainly much exaggerated.

We have seen that, so far as is at present known, Salisbury's army consisted almost entirely of Yorkshiremen, William Stanley being the only Cheshire person of importance who was fighting in his ranks. Stanley's sister, Margaret, married Sir William Troutbeck, and his sister, Elizabeth, married Sir Richard Molineux; and both these knights were killed in the battle, fighting on the side of the Queen. There is nothing to show that they crossed swords with their brother-in-law. On the other hand, his elder brother, Lord Stanley, who, in addition to being brother-in-law of Troutbeck and Molineux, was the son in-law of Salisbury, and was thus intimately connected by marriage with both sides, showed great disinclination to join either, and succeeded in holding aloof.

On the whole it seems that Bloreheath was no worse in this respect than most battles in our Civil Wars; and that the behaviour of the Cheshire gentry compares favourably with that of the aristocracy in other counties, such for instance as that of the Neville family in Yorkshire.

Appendix D gives a few notes as to the living descendants of the heroes of the battle. It does not pretend to be complete. To deal with the subject exhaustively would be a very large undertaking, and far beyond the scope of this little book.

Appendix A

WILLIAM GREGORY'S CHRONICLE, CAMDEN SOCIETY, 1876, VOL. XVII., N.S., 204.

And thys yere was done a grate jornaye at the Blowre Hethe by the Erie of Saulysbury ande the Quenys galentys. And that day the Kynge made VII Knyghtys, fyrste, Syr Robert Molyners, Syr John Daune, Syr Thomas Uttyng, Syr John Brembly, Syr John Stanley, Syr John Grysly, and Syr Rychard Harden; and V of thes Knyghtys were slayne fulle manly in the fylde, and many of the yemonry sore hurte, and a fulle nobylle Knyght, the Lord Audeley, and Syr Thomas Hamdon, Knyght, was the getynge of the fylde, and Thomas Squyer and Counteroller of the Pryncys house fulle sore hurte. And (the) batayle or jornay lastyd all the aftyr none, fro one of the clock tyll V aftyr non, and the chasse lastyd unto VII at the belle in the mornynge. And men were maymyd many one in the Quenys party. There were in the Quenys party V Mi., and in the othyr party V C, a grete wondyr that ever they myght stonde the grete multytude, not ferynge, the Kynge being with yn X myle and the Quene with yn V myle at the Castelle of Egyllyssalle. But the Erie of Saulysbury hadde been i-take, save only a Fryer Austyn schot gonnys alle that nyght in a parke that was at the back syde of the fylde, and by thys mene the Erie come to Duke of Yorke. And in the morowe they found nothyr man ne chylde in that parke but the fryer, and he sayde that for fere he abode in that parke alle that nyght. But in the mornyng, bytwyne the fylde and Chester, Syr John Dawne ys sone[1] that was at home in his fadyr's place hadde worde that hys fadyr was slayne; a-non he raysyd hys tenantys and toke by-syde a lytyl towne i-namyd Torperlay Syr Thomas Nevyle, Syr John Nevyle, and Syr Thomas Haryngdon, and brought hem unto the Castelle of Chester, ande there they a-boode tylle the batayle of Northehampton was done.

Note.—Gregory is not to be trusted as regards the numbers. Five hundred is too small a figure to give for the Yorkists; and also five thousand and fifty for the Lancastrians. But the dispar-ity of numbers, which must have existed, is clearly brought out. The Queen, at Eccleshall, was about ten miles distant, not five. The King was at Coleshill, in Warwickshire, about fifty miles away. I have not been able to identify all the knights mentioned. Molineux and Done are clear enough, Brembly was probably Bromley, and Grysly Gresley; but Utting, Stanley, Harden, and Hamdon are obscure. Thomas, the Controller of the Prince's household, is also a difficulty. He could hardly have been Sir Thomas Fitton, who was not much in favour at Court before the battle.

---

1. John Done was 17 years old when his father died.

Appendix B

Chronicles of Great Britain by Jehan De Waurin.
Rolls Series (1891).Vol. 39, Pp. 269 and 319.

Page 269.

Lors le due d'Yorc oiant ces responces, et sentant quil nestoit pas fort assez pour combattre le roy, il se party dillec si sen alia a Yrlande, et son filz Edouard Comte de la Marche, avec luy les Comtes de Salsebery et de Warewic se misrent en mer et vindrent a Callaix: mais sachies avant que les Comtes dessusdis se departissent du due d'Yorc pour aller vers la mer ilz recontrerent une armee des gens de lo royne dont estoit Capittaine le Seigneur d'Andelay si les combatirent et descomfirent, sicque ilz y morurent ledit Capittaine, les Seigneurs de Charinten et de Kindreton, et y furent prins le baron de Duclay et messire Thomas Fiderne, combien que les gens du due nestoient que quatre cens combatans et ceulz de la royne estoient bien six ou huit mille. Aprez ladite adventure la royne d'Angleterre, de ce moult troublec, fist ses complaintes auz grans seigneurs du conseil du roy, lesquelz lui promisrent tous que pour vengier ceste honte chascun deulz senforceroit de le servir.

Note.—This account of the battle comes out of the chronological order in Waurin's book, and makes it appear to have taken place in 1457. Andelay is evidently Audley, Duclay Dudley, and Fiderne Fitton. The Lord of Kinderton was Sir Hugh Venables; but who Charinten was is not clear. There were Cheshire Lords of Carington and Carincham; but neither of these was killed at Bloreheath

Page 319. After describing the popularity of Warwick, he goes on:

Lequel lors favorisoit le due d'Yorc et sa bende, qui ayant comme dit est la charge de son armée, adcompaignie de environ vingt chincq chevalliers et de six a sept mille hommes deffensables, entre lesquelz navoit pas quarante hommes darmes vint a lencontre du due d'Excestre, si se recontrerent les deux compaignies a Blouher prez dune forest entre la ducie d'Yorc et la Comte Derby. Quant le Comte de Salsbery, le Comte de Warewic et leurs gens aparcheurent droit a ung point de jour larmée d'Excestre et due Seigneur de Beaumont derriere une grant forest haye, dont on ne veiot que les boutz des penons, ilz se misrent a pie a larriere dune forest qui leur faisoit cloture a ung coste, et de lautre avoient mis leur charroy et leur chevaulz lyez les ungz aux autres, et par derriere eulz avoient fait ung bon trenchis pour sceurete, et devant eulz avoient fichie leur peux a la fachon d'Angleterre; et lors quilz se furent mis en ordonnance de bataille, se vindrent rengier devant eulz larmée d'Excestre tous a cheval, et faisoient bien leur conte datraper Warewic et avoir sa compaigine a grant marchie, a pou de traveil et dangier. Lesquelz de Warewic et sa routte aprez eulz estre confessez et mis en etat de morir, baiserent tous la terre sur quoy ilz marchoient, de laquele ilz mengerent, concluant que sur y celle ilz morroient et viveroient: et quant les dis Seigneurs d'Excestre et de Beaumont se veyrent si prez de leurs annemis quilz peuvent employer leur trait ilz se prindrent si onniement a tirer que cestoit horreur, et si radement que partout ou il ataindoit satachoit telement quilz tuerent moult de chevaulz et environ vingt on vingt deux hommes de la compaignie du dit Warewic, et de la compaignie d'Excestre bien de chincq a six cens. Pourquoy ledis d'Excestre demarcherent en recullant environ le trait dun archier, mais pou aprez renchargerent impetueusement sur ledis de Warewic a laquele rencharge moururent, de ceulz d'Excestre environ cent, et des Warewic dix. Alors le Seigneur de Beaumont et sa compaignie, considerans que peu a leur honnour et ancores moins a la prouffit exploitoient a cheval, se misrent a pie environ quatre mille hommes qui se vindrent joindre a la bataille de

74

Warewic ou ilz combatirent main a main bien une grande demye heure, esperans quilz serroient comfortez de leur gens a cheval, lesquelz advisans la resistance quon faisoit a leur gens de pie prindrent le large des champz si laisserent ceulz de pie convenir a leur entreprinse, parquoy ung cheval lier de la routte du Seigneur de Beaumont quy avoit desoubz lui environ chincq cens hommes ce prinst a cryer avec les siens ' Warewic, Warewic! ' et fraper sur la compaignie dudit de Beaumont pourquoy ilz demarcherent ancores en recullant: et lors Warewic parchevant ceste chose crya quon marchast avant, ce qui fut fait, et finablement, furent le Comte de Beaumont et les siens descomfis, si en morut a ceste besongne par le raport des heraulz environ deux mille hommes et de ceulz de Warewic chincquante six, et y furent prins ledit Comte de Beaumont, le Seigneur de Welles et douze autres chevalliers, et le demourant sen fuyrent; laquele bataille fut ou mois de Septembre trois ou quatre jours avant la feste de St. Michiel.

Note.—This interesting and circumstantial account contains some obvious errors. Bloreheath is not on the borders of Yorkshire and Derbyshire. Warwick was not present with his father, Salisbury; nor were Exeter and Beaumont and Welles fighting on the other side. For Exeter we may substitute Audley, and for Beaumont Dudley.

Appendix C

The old roads over Bloreheath, which were superseded by new ones laid out under the powers given by the Turnpike Act of 1768 (9 George III. 55), and the Act for inclosing Bloreheath (passed in 1773, and acted upon in 1775).

1. *The Main Road Leading from the Loggerheads to Shifford's Bridge.* In the year 1587 the Manor of Tyrley was divided into three parts of equal value, one of which was allotted to Sir Gilbert Gerard, one to Alice widow of Reginald Corbet, and the other to James Skrymsher, they being the persons who were each entitled to an undivided third part of it.

This partition was effected by a writ issued by the Sheriff, in which the various parcels are fully set out.[1] The site of the present Rowney farm was then occupied by a wood called the Little Rowney; and through this wood the road passed, coming out on to Bloreheath near the boundary between the Rowney and Blore Hall farms.

To Sir Gilbert Gerard was awarded by the writ the Eastern-most portion of the heath, and his Eastern boundary against Blore Hall, or Netherblore, was "along the road leading to Drayton as far as a certain place called Hales Dale." Hales Dale is, of course, the valley of the Wemberton Brook; and the name was given to it to distinguish it from the more Northern val-

---

1. There are two originals of this document, one in Latin and one in English, at Tunstall, neither quite perfect. There is an early copy at Oakley.
2. It was not a good name, being likely to be confused with the "Lloyd Drumble" which is much nearer to Hales; and is now quite disused.

ley, called Blore Dale.[3] It is clear, therefore, that the old road to Drayton ran along the Eastern edge of the heath as far as the Wemberton Brook. From the point where it came to the brook, a road led on in a Southerly direction, up the hill to Blore village. But the road to Drayton made a sharp turn to the light, and followed the brook down as far as Bloreheath mill pool; where it crossed the brook, and followed more or less the line of the present main road down to its junction with the road leading from Mucclestone to Market Drayton. [4]

From this point it kept to its present line, forming the Southern boundary of Shifford's Grange, as it did in the thirteenth century.[4]

There is not much to be seen of the old road along the Wemberton Brook; the brook has been diverted, and the ground levelled, for irrigation purposes. And I think that between 1768 and 1838, when the tithe map was made, the dam of the mill pool was raised, and the pool enlarged so as almost to cover the site of the old road. The road must have gone along the North side of the pool, crossing the brook just below it. But the entrance to the mill seems to have been on the other side of the valley, where a depression marks the line of the lane that led to it.

The old road, therefore, made a considerable bend; and we can well believe that in 1768 it was found to be "deep and ruinous," and also "narrow and incommodious," to adopt the wording of the Act of Parliament.

The obvious remedy was to divert the road and make a new and direct one across the waste of Bloreheath, which would cut off the bend. And accordingly the Act provided that a road forty feet wide might be made, and that no compensation should be paid to the owners of the waste land. The Inclosure Act gave power to increase the width of the road from forty feet to sixty. And in this way the present straight road across Bloreheath came into being, and the steep banks below the mill were cut down

---

3. Direct proof is wanting; but it must have been so, unless we are to suppose that the traffic went all the way round by Blore village.
4. Charter of 1447, quoting an earlier one of about 1295, at Tunstall.

and the hollow between them filled up. A large gravel pit was also opened at this point, for the reparation of the roads of the parish.

The Act of 1768 also provided for the erection of a cart bridge over the Tern, instead of the ancient narrow horse bridge. This bridge still remains; but the approaches to it have been straightened and improved, so that it now makes an awkward angle, and is not in a true line with the road.

2. *The Mucclestone Lane.* This is referred to in the Writ of Partition, where it is called the "Common lane." At that time it ran through open heath land all the way from Sandy Lane to the Mucclestone boundary, and had no fence on either side of it. Its line does not seem to have been much altered.

3. *The Road which Crosses the Main Road Below Bloreheath Mill.* This was set out by the Commissioners appointed under the Inclosure Act of 1773. The Northern portion of it follows the boundary line between the Skrymsher and Corbet shares of Bloreheath. The Southern portion leads straight to the point from which roads diverge, to Blore and Hales respectively.

4. *The Straight Drive to Oakley from the Mucclestone Lane.* This passes over the North-western portion of Bloreheath, and was made about the year 1714. This piece of land was bought by Sir John Chetwode from William Church (whose ancestor had purchased it from the Corbets) in February, 1713-4; and the new road across it is shown on the Oakley estate map of 1715. The old road seems to have followed the Wemberton Brook down from Bloreheath Mill, past Daisey Lake, and to have come out into the present back road to Oakley Hall.

5. *The Road up the Wemberton Brook Valley past Netherblore.* There seems to have been a road up this valley, from Bloreheath Mill to Netherblore, which there divided. One road kept to the right, past the "Cold Comfort" farm, and through the woods to Fair Oak and Eccleshall. This road can be easily traced. The other road, or track, which branched off to the left at Netherblore, followed the line of a watercourse dividing the Little Rowney Wood from the Great Rowney, and led into the road from Drayton to Newcastle, a little below the Loggerheads Inn. The line of this road is marked by an existing footpath. The ground over which it goes is rather stiff and low-lying; and the route was less convenient than the alternative one across the dry gravelly land of Bloreheath. But, in the days when robbers abounded and travellers liked to be unobtrusive, it had the merit of being well-screened from observation.

6. *The Lane from Blore Village to Sandy Lane.* This is still the road from Blore to the corner of the road leading to Hales. The Western part of it, which has been superseded by the newer road leading to Bloreheath Mill, used to go straight on past two cottages, which still remain; and it joined the main road between Sandy lane and Bloreheath Mill, near where the new Bloreheath farm stands. Part of the old lane still remains, but some of it has been thrown into the adjoining fields.

7. *Footpath from Blore to Mucclestone.* The Court Rolls of the Manor tell us that the existing footpath across Netherblore and Bloreheath towards Mucclestone is ancient, and was for the convenience of persons attending Mucclestone Church. The entry relating to it is dated 27th March, 1553.

Appendix D

1. *Descendants of the Earl of Salisbury.* There do not seem to be any in the male line. The Stanleys of Knowsley, are descended from his daughter Eleanor. He had five other daughters, who may possibly have living representatives.

The Marquis of Abergavenny is descended from Edward Neville, Salisbury's brother; and various families can claim descent from his sisters. His sister Eleanor (by her second husband, Henry Percy Earl of Northumberland, son of Hotspur who was killed at Shrewsbury in 1403), is the ancestress of the Dukes of Northumberland. This Eleanor, through her daughter Katherine, has for descendants the Earl of Wilton, the Egertons of Oulton, the Warburtons of Arley, the Wilbrahams of Rode, the Corbets of Adderley, the Tarletons of Breakspears, and other allied families.

Another sister, Cecily Duchess of York, has, through her elder daughter Anne Duchess of Exeter, numerous descendants, whose pedigrees have been worked out by the writers on Royal descents.

2. *Descendants of Sir John Conyers.* Sir John is at present represented by the Countess of Yarborough, who is Baroness Conyers in her own right; and her sister the Countess of Powis.

3. *Descendants of Sir William Stanley.* It does not appear that Sir William Stanley has any living descendants. He had a son

William, who married the heiress of Tatton, Joan daughter of Sir Geoffrey Massv. They had a daughter and heiress named Joan, who married Sir Richard Brereton. The grandson of these latter, another Richard Brereton, died childless in 1598, and settled Tatton upon Sir Thomas Egerton, the Lord Chancellor, whose descendants still hold it.

The Stanleys of Alderley are descended from Sir William's younger brother, John.

4. *Issue of Lord Audley.* Lord Audley has numerous descendants. The peerage continued in direct male descent until 1777; and on the death of the eighteenth baron it passed to his sister's son George Thicknesse, who took the name of Touchet.

At present the barony is in abeyance between two co-heiresses, the Hon. Mary and the Hon. Emily Thicknesse Touchet, who are both unmarried and live in Hampshire.

But the local connection of the family with Staffordshire, Cheshire, and Shropshire was severed in the 16th century. The son of the Lord Audley who turned Yorkist and fought against his father's friends, rebelled against Henry VII., was captured at Blackheath in 1497, and beheaded on Tower Hill. His son was restored in blood; but the family fortunes declined. The Manor of Buglawton was surrendered to the Crown in 1535.[1] Newhall was alienated also in the reign of Henry VIII.[2]

The Manor of Hawkstone was held by Sir Rowland Hill in 1559; so it would seem that Red Castle had gone from the Audleys before that date.[3] And Harwood (p.99) says that Audley was sold to Sir Gilbert Gerard in 1577,[4] by George Lord Audley, who was created Earl of Castlehaven in 1617. The last Earl of Castlehaven died in 1777, when the old barony of Audley passed, as already said, to George Thicknesse. This is an old Staffordshire

---

1. Ormerod's *Cheshire*, Vol. III.
2. Lysons, *Magna Britannia*, Vol. II. Part II.
3. There is an early copy of the settlement of his large estates upon his relatives, made by Sir Rowland at this time, amongst the papers at Tunstall. He settled Hawkstone upon his cousin Humphrey Hill of Adderley in fee.
4. This is corroborated by a Court Roll of that Manor at Aqualate, dated 1586. Sir Gilbert was then lord of the Manor.

name, connected with Audley and the neighbouring township of Balterley from very early times till 1790, when Ralph Thicknesse sold Balterley Hall. The family held land in Tunstall (near Market Drayton), and Tyrley, between 1387 and 1586.[5]

Sir Philip Walhouse Chetwode represents the Touchets of Nether Whitley, co. Chester, his ancestor Philip Chetwode of Oakley having married Hester Touchet the heiress of that family, in 1664. Sir Philip is not, so far as I know, lineally descended from Lord Audley, but from his cousin and contemporary Thomas Touchet.

Many local families can claim descent from Lord Audley through females. His daughter Anne[6] married Hugh Done of Oulton, and was an ancestress of the Egertons of Oulton, and of the families connected with them.

Anne Touchet, sister of the Lord Audley who sold Audley and became Earl of Castlehaven, married Thomas Brooke, of Norton Priory co. Chester; and from her are descended the present Sir Richard Brooke of Norton, and collateral branches of his family, and also the Wilbrahams of Delamere, Lathom, and Rode, who have several times intermarried with the Brookes.

5. *Sir Hugh de Venables*, Baron of Kinderton, left no descendants, being succeeded in his property by a cousin who was his heir.

6. *Sir Robert del Booth*, of Dunham, is represented by the Earl of Stamford and Warrington. The Chetwodes, Colonel Cotes of Pitchford, the Bougheys of Aqualate, and Mr. Brooke of Haughton, are also descended from him in the female line.

7. *Sir Thomas Dutton* of Dutton, has no living descendants. Ormerod I.

8. *Sir John Egerton* was the ancestor of the Egertons of Oulton, and grandfather of the Sir John Egerton who married Elizabeth Done, the grand-daughter of James Lord Audley.

---

5. Deeds at Tunstall.
6. Her first husband was Sir Thomas Dutton, killed at Bloreheath.

9. *Sir John Legh*, of Knutsford Booths, had descendants. The male line came to an end about 1700, Ruth, the heiress, marrying Thomas Pennington. Their issue Mill survives. Ormerod I.

10. *Sir Richard Molynenx* was the ancester of the Earls of Sefton.

11. *Sir William Troutbeck* of Dunham-on-the-Hill,[7] left a great-grand-daughter and heiress, who married Sir John Talbot, ancestor of the Earls of Shrewsbury. Ormerod II.

12. *Sir Thomas Fitt*on of Gawsworth, had no children, and was succeeded by his brother. The Fittons are now extinct in the male line, and Gawsworth belongs to the Earl of Harrington, who can claim descent from them through females (Earwaker's *East Cheshire*, vol. II.).

---

7. Described in the Herald's Visitation pedigree of 1589 as of Prynes Castle in Wirral.

LEONAUR

ALSO FROM LEONAUR
AVAILABLE IN SOFTCOVER OR HARDCOVER WITH DUST JACKET

IRON TIMES WITH THE GUARDS *by An O. E. (G. P. A. Fildes)*—The Experiences of an Officer of the Coldstream Guards on the Western Front During the First World War.

THE GREAT WAR IN THE MIDDLE EAST: 1 *by W. T. Massey*—The Desert Campaigns & How Jerusalem Was Won---two classic accounts in one volume.

THE GREAT WAR IN THE MIDDLE EAST: 2 *by W. T. Massey*—Allenby's Final Triumph.

SMITH-DORRIEN *by Horace Smith-Dorrien*—Isandlwhana to the Great War.

1914 *by Sir John French*—The Early Campaigns of the Great War by the British Commander.

GRENADIER *by E. R. M. Fryer*—The Recollections of an Officer of the Grenadier Guards throughout the Great War on the Western Front.

BATTLE, CAPTURE & ESCAPE *by George Pearson*—The Experiences of a Canadian Light Infantryman During the Great War.

DIGGERS AT WAR *by R. Hugh Knyvett & G. P. Cuttriss*—"Over There" With the Australians by R. Hugh Knyvett and Over the Top With the Third Australian Division by G. P. Cuttriss. Accounts of Australians During the Great War in the Middle East, at Gallipoli and on the Western Front.

HEAVY FIGHTING BEFORE US *by George Brenton Laurie*—The Letters of an Officer of the Royal Irish Rifles on the Western Front During the Great War.

THE CAMELIERS *by Oliver Hogue*—A Classic Account of the Australians of the Imperial Camel Corps During the First World War in the Middle East.

RED DUST *by Donald Black*—A Classic Account of Australian Light Horsemen in Palestine During the First World War.

THE LEAN, BROWN MEN *by Angus Buchanan*—Experiences in East Africa During the Great War with the 25th Royal Fusiliers—the Legion of Frontiersmen.

THE NIGERIAN REGIMENT IN EAST AFRICA *by W. D. Downes*—On Campaign During the Great War 1916-1918.

THE 'DIE-HARDS' IN SIBERIA *by John Ward*—With the Middlesex Regiment Against the Bolsheviks 1918-19.

LEONAUR

ALSO FROM LEONAUR

AVAILABLE IN SOFTCOVER OR HARDCOVER WITH DUST JACKET

THE 9TH—THE KING'S (LIVERPOOL REGIMENT) IN THE GREAT WAR 1914 - 1918 *by Enos H. G. Roberts*—Mersey to mud—war and Liverpool men.

THE GAMBARDIER *by Mark Severn*—The experiences of a battery of Heavy artillery on the Western Front during the First World War.

FROM MESSINES TO THIRD YPRES *by Thomas Floyd*—A personal account of the First World War on the Western front by a 2/5th Lancashire Fusilier.

THE IRISH GUARDS IN THE GREAT WAR - VOLUME 1 *by Rudyard Kipling*—Edited and Compiled from Their Diaries and Papers—The First Battalion.

THE IRISH GUARDS IN THE GREAT WAR - VOLUME 1 *by Rudyard Kipling*—Edited and Compiled from Their Diaries and Papers—The Second Battalion.

ARMOURED CARS IN EDEN *by K. Roosevelt*—An American President's son serving in Rolls Royce armoured cars with the British in Mesopatamia & with the American Artillery in France during the First World War.

CHASSEUR OF 1914 *by Marcel Dupont*—Experiences of the twilight of the French Light Cavalry by a young officer during the early battles of the great war in Europe.

TROOP HORSE & TRENCH *by R.A. Lloyd*—The experiences of a British Lifeguardsman of the household cavalry fighting on the western front during the First World War 1914-18.

THE EAST AFRICAN MOUNTED RIFLES *by C.J. Wilson*—Experiences of the campaign in the East African bush during the First World War.

THE LONG PATROL *by George Berrie*—A Novel of Light Horsemen from Gallipoli to the Palestine campaign of the First World War.

THE FIGHTING CAMELIERS *by Frank Reid*—The exploits of the Imperial Camel Corps in the desert and Palestine campaigns of the First World War.

STEEL CHARIOTS IN THE DESERT *by S. C. Rolls*—The first world war experiences of a Rolls Royce armoured car driver with the Duke of Westminster in Libya and in Arabia with T.E. Lawrence.

WITH THE IMPERIAL CAMEL CORPS IN THE GREAT WAR *by Geoffrey Inchbald*—The story of a serving officer with the British 2nd battalion against the Senussi and during the Palestine campaign.

Lightning Source UK Ltd.
Milton Keynes UK
UKOW04n2305070715

254774UK00001B/5/P